Norbert Braun

GROSS NATIONAL HAPPINESS

VERSUS

PREDATORY CAPITALISM

**An Attempt to Counteract
the Western Economic
"Twilight of the Gods"**

**Bibliographic Information
of the German National Library
(Deutsche Nationalbibliothek)**

The German National Library
lists this publication
in the German National Bibliography.
For detailed bibliographic data
please refer to: http://dnb.d-nb.de

**Original title: Bruttosozialglück statt Raubtierkapitalismus
Copyright: 2010 Norbert Braun
Printed and published by: Books on Demand GmbH,
Norderstedt
ISBN: 978-3-8391-9088-3**

Translation by: Norbert Braun

**Copyright: 2011 Norbert Braun
Printed and published by: Books on Demand GmbH
Norderstedt
ISBN: 978-3-8423-3736-7**

CONTENTS

FOREWORD

Some twenty years ago, the events were already emerging which have now become reality.

Many people to whom I spoke about this did not want to know the facts and brushed my arguments aside.

So I addressed myself to the German Federal Government in an attempt to place my Asian experience at their disposal. Especially the last two Federal Chancellors expressed their interest in my suggestions. .As a result, a vivid and mutually beneficial exchange of thoughts took place over a period of ten years.

Many of my ideas and suggestions found entry into German politics. However, there is a great gap between the understanding of a Federal Chancellor and the bureaucrats who are supposed to carry out the ideas.

Unfortunately, Germany lacks the total performance dedication of the Asian systems.

It has become much more difficult to remain on top of the league.

PREFACE

We are currently experiencing a phase of global changes. The white man and his superiority is being replaced by the new Asian superpower.

Gradually, we are experiencing the "Twilight of the Gods" of the industrial and economic order created by the West.

The EC did not succeed in maintaining the industrial activities reserved by the Chinese.

The financial and industrial superiority of the Asians is relentlessly carried through and is already undermining our financial basis.

The growth of the Gross National Product is no longer a suitable means of orientation.

In this book, the Author is trying to replace the Gross National Product by Gross National **HAPPINESS**.

Striving towards happiness could replace the strive for economic growth.

With this attitude, the diminishing resources of our planet would be safeguarded, and mankind would regard happiness as the measure of all things.

INTRODUCTION:

THE GROSS NATIONAL PRODUCT -

DOES IT STILL MAKE SENSE ?

For more than a century, our lives have been dominated by the growth of the Gross National Product.

Now the Western countries are gradually losing the race for economic domination on this planet.

China and India are creating an army of scientists, inventors, engineers and product developers every year. They take care of all Western new product and technological developments and concentrate on the improvement and further development of these inventions.

Today China is ruled by a Government of scientists. They unterstand the importance of bypassing the Western countries technologically. Many fine Western developments are not yet protected in all markets.

Chinese institutions try to be faster with the patent applications. Alternatively, they patent their improvements.

In reality, this means that Western industry has lost the game. Western industrialists are not allowed to exploit their own inventions and developments.

In Western Governments, lawyers have discovered a new way to earn their bread. Yet their education does not allow them to unterstand the complex Chinese strategies. They have no real chance in this game. They can only play the brave role of eternal victims.

China has been the center of the economical and civilized world. Step by step they are regaining their traditional position. The dominance of the West is a passing event.

The Chinese politicians are aware that the future will be strongly influenced by the shortage of raw materials.

China has invested time and effort to create a close co-operation and financial dependence with the countries of the Third World. Loans have been granted in exchange for exploitation rights off-shore as well as on land.

The mountain of money which China has earned in the West has been well invested to secure the many raw materials essential for long-term industrial strength and financial dominance.

The West may have to limit its growth due to the shortage of raw materials. Objectives and planning have to be tuned to the evolution. It may be essential to turn a disadvantage into an advantage. New horizons are required.

Scientist-based Governments have a formidable advantage in creating the industries of tomorrow. Their rate of the right visionary decisions will be much higher than that of the lawyer-dominated Governments. They will gradually lose competitiveness.

It appears that many polititions are aware of this evolution. They start to concentrate on enriching themselves with all available means rather than shining with political merits.

**The age of the Gross National Product philosophy
is coming to an end.**

**The new philosophy of Gross National HAPPINESS
has to take its place.**

GROSS NATIONAL HAPPINESS -

WHAT DOES IT MEAN ?

A German Government Minister explained recently that it would be better to have millions of workers working at half wage level rather than having no jobs at all.

Rich countries eagerly compete for the jobs of any industrialist. In the medium- and long-term we shall experience a globalization of wages.

Already today, China is the factory of the world. They will determine the wage standard of tomorrow.

With an average wage of US-$ 400 or 500 a Chinese migrant worker can afford a new house and to be the major bread winner of a large family.

With this income level a Western worker will have to queue up for a public meal or public food in an alternative supermarket (in Germany, welfare organisations collect perishable food from supermarkets and restaurants and sell it in shops at very low prices to the underprivileged). Those people cannot afford a roof over their head.

This development, asks for the creation of a society which provides a decent bourgeois living at Asian wage levels.

The moment has come to replace the gross national product by gross national happiness and to create a society with a high life quality for everybody. The hunt for a limitless growth of the gross national product leads to the exhaustion of the resources of our globe at an unreasonable speed.

The change of human values will take a long time. We should start now with the pursuit of happiness and the pursuit of improving the happiness of our neighbours.

How can we achieve and improve happiness of the growing underprivileged sections of society ?

Interesting and exciting tasks for as many people as possible is perhaps the most important source of national happiness.

The creation of products, artistic expression, the welfare of natural food production, sport and maintenance of health will create more job satisfaction and human dignity.

The protection of human dignity has to become an important pillar of human rights. The right of a job as the backbone of human dignity has to overrule the relentless pursuit for profits.

In Southern China and Corea I have seen that many jobs are maintained to avoid unemployment. There they leave the relentless rationalization to Western industrialists who are prepared to create thousands of victims in their relentless pursuit for mega profits.

The efficient use of Internet Marketing on an international level can provide a global presence. At the same time it provides the building-up of a hard currency stock.

Concerning the building of homes, Chinese and Indian prices have to be achieved. This requires large-scale projects and very precise planning. At the same time, an industry has to be built up to supply the materials for the construction projects. Here as well the Asian price level has to be achieved.

The availability of homes at Asian price levels is probably the most important key factor for long-term success.

A Complementary Economy (CE) provides the chance to build up a whole industry which tunes itself to Asian price level.

OBJECTIVES

OF

GROSS NATIONAL HAPPINESS

Happiness is strongly coloured and influenced by the personality of each individual.

The following elements may contribute to the satisfaction and happiness of most individuals:

- An interesting profession or job which mobilizes your personality and gives you deep satisfaction

- Personal dignity and respect in your environment.

- Enjoyment of health and fitness even at a very advanced age.

- Job security and reliable sources of income as long as mental and physical power permit.

- Reliable pensions for the time after.

- Enjoyment of the countless delicacies of the many cuisines of the world.

- Promotion of intellectual capacities and activities.

- Creation of happy families and enjoyment of happy family lives.

- Promotion of communication between people with different education levels.

- Promotion of communication with people of different cultures and spiritual believes to make life richer.

- Globalization of culture and benefiting from selected elements of other cultures and civilizations.

- Maintenance of works of art, civilization and culture.

- Promotion of communication with our fellow creatures like animals and plants.

- Creation of life opportunities and welfare for our fellow creatures.

Happiness is not achieved by competing with your neighbours for owning a more attractive car or enjoying a more glamorous holiday.

**We have to develop ways of happiness
which protect the dwindling resources of our planet.**

1   LIFE QUALITY FOR EVERYBODY

In a CE life quality is most likely higher than in the First Economy..

Jobs in major factories will become more frequent in Asia, but dwindle to a trickle in Western countries.

A CE will never transfer jobs to China or rationalize jobs away to satisfy the instinct of mega profits for a chosen few. The human aspect will prevail.

Humanity will be the alternative to predatory capitalism.

Most likely, the CE will be in competition with the dynamic Asian economies right from the start.

This competition requires a considerable creativity and the will to persevere against tough Asian competitors.

The complacency and arrogance of Eastern European socialist economies will not have a chance to develop. A day-to-day battle of wits and cleverness has to be fought out. This will speed up evolution.

The challenge to remain globally competitive to Asia's rapidly progressing economies will challenge the intellectual capacities of everybody in a CE.

Everybody has to broaden their mind at all times and to be open to new horizons. This necessity will improve the quality of life much more than anything else.

We are at a point of evolution where the large industrial dinosaurs are on the decline.

The highly flexible "mammals" of the CE will be forced to take their place to ensure survival.

2 ENJOYMENT OF FOOD

In some countries, e. g. in China, the enjoyment of food has the status of a religion. France has a similar point of view.

The enormous variety of tasty dishes from many regions raise a meal to a life quality event which may be enjoyed for a larger part of the day. A dish may be a work of art and is often presented as such.

In countries like China 60 million people died of hunger due to mismanagement. The bodies of senior people still carry signs of long periods of malnutrition.

A large table full of many small and tasteful dishes is often the centerpiece of weekend enjoyment. It brings together the members of a larger family or a group of friends to enjoy fine food and an intensive exchange of experiences and points of view. It promotes the community feeling of a family or group and develops solidarity.

Asia, Europe and the two Americas offer an incredible variety of thousands of fine dishes. Their enjoyment is an important element of life quality.

Dwindling energy resources may render it more and more difficult to spend holidays in faraway places and to sample fine foods.

People in China, France, Indonesia and Vietnam have learned to turn low cost ingredients into delicious dishes by using the wealth of spices.

Opening up the market of a CE for the immense variety of dishes which the global community provides may create an enormous number of new jobs.

The ingredients of the vast variety of foods have to be produced. They create unlimited opportunities for many thousands of small companies.

**Food supply is a key challenge in a declining economy.
Why not solving the problem in the most enjoyable way ?**

3   INFLUENCE OF FOOD ON LIFE EXPECTANCY

Health conscious people in China always had a close and thorough look at the effects of food on organs, cells and the chemical processes of the body.

This is a very useful approach which is mostly neglected in Western food tradition.

Many foods may have an excellent taste but are absolutely unhealthy. Their enjoyment will cause cardio-vascular diseases and cancer in the long run.

Many traditional nutriments are cherished, which may go back to the age of the Romans. Life expectancy was 40 on average at that time. Today:s living conditions allow for a life expectancy of 100 years.

Many tasty nutriments you may only enjoy on rare occasions. The many national cuisines of the global community will offer you an abundance of alternatives. They will enrich your choices and increase food enjoyment.

The conservative approach to food should be abandoned. People take great care in supplying the motor of their car with the right oil and petrol. The sophisticated complex chemical processes in their bodies require far greater care in the choice of food input.

It pays to make a selection of your 100 favourite dishes and analyse their effect on the chemical, cellular and cardio-vascular processes of your body.

With your mental and autosuggestive capabilities you can certainly create a positive influence on the well-functioning of your body processes.

For a CE, the maintenance and health of a person's body
up to a high age is of key importance.

4   ASIAN HEALTH MAINTENANCE

Asia is immensely rich in ways and methods to improve your health in a natural way. The alternative starts wich Ayurveda and ends with Zen.

Everybody has to make their own choice according to their interests and preferences.

The improvement of the mental and spiritual strength as well as the immune system are very vital for life prolongation.

These are key factors to reduce medical costs and to increase the span of a useful working life.

A CE has to limit social costs as much as possible. The vast majority can contribute to the success in a new economic world. The care of people who need public help should be as small as possible.

The CE has to offer a wide range of programmes which promote Asian health and longevity strategies.

TV, PC and face-to-face training offer such a choice.

The systematic development of mental and physical strength is a key issue for the long-term success of a CE.

The maintenance of public health is extremely important for the financial well-being of a CE.

It is, therefore, essential to control that everybody participates. The evolution of global competition requires a constant development of mental and physical capabilities.

The situation requires a permanent improvement of competitiveness.

5   MENTAL AND PHYSICAL FITNESS

Mental and physical deterioration is accelerated if senior citizens do not have an interesting job.

Mind and body have to be occupied with interesting activities all the time.

Mental and physical fitness of the entire population will reduce social costs dramatically.

Individuals have to be trained and encouraged to organize their own fitness programme.

For individuals who have a less active mind an integration in team activity and team effort is essential.

The fitness and working capacity of the senior population is an extremely valuable asset which has to be carefully maintained. They have a wealth of experience which has to be re-activated with intelligent programmes.

Activation and mobilization of the creativity, enthusiasm and working discipline can mean the difference between prosperity and decline for a country.

Longevity as well as mental and physical fitness up to an age of 100 have to replace the deterioration of human capacities.

It may be necessary to apply subtle pressure on the less active section of the population and to organize mountain walks and bike trips to beauty spots.

We have to remember that many of the great achievements of mankind, e.g. the works of art of Michelangelo, the philosophical works of Sokrates or Tagore etc., have been created at a senior age.

**We cannot afford
to neglect the working capacity of senior citizens.**

6 PROMOTION OF INTELLECTUAL CAPACITIES AND ACTIVITIES

A CE has to provide and create many jobs for senior people who are called "Troisième Age" in France.

One of the main objectives has to be to maintain mental fitness beyond the age of 100.

The brain has to be used like a muscle to prevent mental diseases and neglect of brain activities.

Brain activities are just as important as remuneration and are a key element of personality and self expression.

Everybody has to be integrated into intellectual activities at his or her choice.

This can be done by means of E-learning or face-to-face instruction.

The working faculties of each individual have to be maintained. The very high costs for treatment and care of mental neglect have to be minimized.

It is better to invest these immense funds into new products and the realization of important projects.

The promotion of brain training, knowledge and skills should start immediately after entering the CE.

To re-start an extensive brain activity after decades of neglect is possible, but very cumbersome.

A reasonable solution could be to invest 50 % of your efforts in learning new skills and expanding professional knowledge. The other 50 % could be spent in learning new intellectual activities to improve life quality and to broaden your mind.

The continuous opening-up of new horizons and the maintenance of a life-long learning process are very important elements of gross national happiness.

It may be necessary that a friendly, gentle pressure and motivation efforts have to be applied to people who have an inclination to comfort.

I am sure that they will be grateful in the end.

7   TALENT PROMOTION AT KINDERGARTEN AGE

The most precious resources which a CE possesses are the creativity, talent and diligence of its people.

It is very important to start developing the talents of the next generation at a very young age.

The potential of very talented outstanding young people has to be realized at kindergarten age. The early school age should be a further opportunity.

Around outstanding talents employment clusters can be created. It is an opportunity to build up product groups which are related to outstanding talents.

Around sport talents a production of sport products could emerge. Around musical talents a production of musical instruments could be developed.

The systematic creation of competence centers creates new specialized productions which require a high level of skill.

This is essential to maintain jobs over long periods of time. The emphasis has to be placed on creating as many jobs as possible.

Many jobs would, of course, disappear in a profit optimizing production. Many people would lose their jobs.

But not everybody can be a genius. As many jobs as possible have to be created and maintained for people with normal intelligence.

Such responsibilites create human dignity and an identity in their environment.

Performance-oriented humanity should prevail.

8   CREATION OF HAPPY FAMILIES

The average man or woman enjoys a much higher life quality if he or she has the right partner at his or her side to share life with him or her.

With most singles, it is difficult to discover really happy faces. The frequent change of partners does not really lead to a deep happiness of the soul.

The responsibilty for a family increases the motivation to create outstanding achievements.

With an advancing age, it becomes extremely difficult to find suitable partners. A long period of frustration begins. Life quality is reduced dramatically.

Everybody is a member of a group with similar or compatible interests.

If a group realizes that a member has problems to find a suitable marriage partner, they should give a helping hand.

They should use their contacts outside the group and present suitable marriage partners until success has been achieved.

The happiness of deep love between two partners and the deep satisfaction and life quality which has its source in this union should be a right in a society which promotes happiness.

The wisdom of experienced members of the group should prevent marriage between partners who will prove to be unsuitable in the long run.

**Marriage-based deep personal happiness
is a key factor of gross national happiness.
Its promotion is certainly worthwhile.**

9   CREATION OF HOMES AT PAYABLE PRICES

In Germany the start of a new economic life began by removing the ruins and re-constructing towns.

This is a very efficient way to create many jobs and to start a new economy on a larger scale.

The construction of homes on a larger scale reduces production costs dramatically.

The re-construction of entire German cities proves that you can build towns with highly motivated non-professional staff.

An organized distribution of professional know-how is, of course, beneficial.

Our economic system has been created by the wealthy for the wealthy. In an economical system under pressure the wealthy will implement solutions to maintain the good life for the top 10 % of society. The other 90 % of society have to rely upon themselves to create a quality life.

Our currency system is ideally placed on the value of gold or hard currency.

The people who create a new economy have only their labour available. The value of labour is a noble alternative to gold. Vouchers are issued which have the value of labour as a basis. Thus the value of labour receives purchasing power and creates new opportunities to earn a living for the millions of victims of industrial migration to Asia and the millions of jobs which have been rationalized away.

Their motivation to work and their energy to progress in life are the most precious assets which they can make available.

In Bangla Desh, Argentine, Brazil and Switzerland well-functioning systems of self-help of underprivileged communities have already been in existence for a long time.

In our society, the social status of a person is expressed by his or her work and profession. If you take this away you destroy the backbone of a human's existance.

Many fine people who have been made superfluous fall into a deep depression and decide to terminate their existance on the rails of a train.

I myself have experienced how a Director of a Marketing Department finished his life in a traffic accident after he had been made redundant.

A society which integrates the up to 80's in its working life and creates working conditions for senior personell can dramatically reduce social costs.

This is an important job to get prices down to Asian level. This step reduces the need for high taxes and improves the quality of life.

In Western societies the prices of homes are often inflated and much too high. This makes inflated wages essential to pay for inflated houses.

The construction of new towns is a unique opportunity to get the prices of homes down to Asian level. This is an essential step to become more competitive and to succeed against Asian competition.

The creation of new towns is an ideal means to achieve full employment in a region.

A CE should be tax-free or have very low taxes. It creates platforms to find employment for the unfortunate who do not find jobs in an economy with shrinking wages and shrinking job opportunities.

After the war factories in Germany were full of experts above 70 years of age. They did beautiful jobs in the re-construction of towns and industries.

This gave them dignity and an important place in society.
It improved their mental and physical fitness enormously.

10   RELIABLE PENSIONS FOR THE TIME AFTER

A pension begin at the Inka age of 80 makes pensions safe and payable. It creates stability even in a period of the economic decline of the West.

A basic pension Western nations will always be able to honour.

The West suffers from being bypassed by important financial currents. The decline of some economies is balanced by the boom in other economies.

A CE has to aim at earning at least one third of its income in the booming economies like China, India and Brazil. Other nations will join the strong growth club.

Great efforts should be made to increase the share of the boom countries from one third to one half.

The marketing and business-to-business opportunities of the Internet should create the working base to reach the booming countries at the other end of the world.

Alternatives should be created to the very successful global marketing structures. This creates a great number of new job opportunities which can be fulfilled by senior people.

This, of course, requires a very professional training structure and an atmosphere of friendliness and excellent service to develop solid operation bases in a very competitive world.

One third of the income should be earned in the larger economic community and one third in the home state.

It is very important to be fit for the rapidly changing world.

11 THE INKA SYSTEM - PENSION AT 80

The Inka have proved that by leading a healthy life in connection with sufficient fitness excercises pension at 80 is a realistic solution.

The scientific efforts in the field of anti-ageing, the fitness efforts of wide sections of the population make a pension at 80 possible already now for the major part of the population.

A Pension at 80 is always payable.

Pension at 80 can already be introduced now to the mentally and physically active section of the population.

Millions prefer to continue their jobs. Our merciless system pushes them out of their work which represents their social status.

The premature removal from their social status accelerates the physical decline of a personality and often reduces his or her life span dramatically.

The step-by-step return to an Inka-style working life cycle would solve the financial problem of pension payment.

Society has to make considerable efforts to replace the millions of jobs which we have lost to Asian economic expansion and in the advance of technology.

The problems of unemployment could be solved at the same time.

The wealthy aim at interest rates of 25 %. Solving the problems of pensioners is not profitable or not profitable enough. These profits can only be made in booming economies.

**Only CE activities can present solutions
which prevent precious human capital
from being wasted.**

12   LIFE QUALITY FOR VERY SENIOR PEOPLE

Predatory capitalism has thrown valuable, hard working and honest people away like junk.

I have experienced myself that capable Managers were very shocked by the cold inhuman handling of their fate through the top Management.

The rough handling as human junk has been very humiliating for them. It destroyed their pride and their identity in human society.

They had not developed alternatives to occupy their talents and saw no other way out than to commit suicide.

The most important contribution which a CE can make to human society is the human, compassionate and warmhearted management of the talents of their participants.

A continuous creation of job opportunities for senior citizens is an essential service which has to be provided.

A CE has to place people in its center.

Job opportunities have to be created for people who would not have a remote chance in the First Economy.

Global Internet Marketing is a very wide field where many senior people could find very exciting job opportunities. A substantial part of this key activity should be open to senior people.

The enormous flexibility of mind which is required is a constant challenge and keeps the mind top-fit.

The very important constant learning process will increase life quality and the feeling of self-esteem and dignity of senior people.

Senior people who are more gifted in manual work can participate in the production of products for which the Internet Marketing colleagues have to develop new markets.

13   PROMOTION OF COMMUNICATION WITH OTHER CULTURES

The sytematic conquest of most essential industries through China and other Asian nations has changed its financial currents. Money is becoming scarce in many Western regions.

A CE has to adapt to the enormously changed circumstances.

The remaining patches of a high standard of living have to be thoroughly developed. The thorough exploitation of each region with a promising economical strength becomes a necessity.

The pressure of Asian competition makes a thorough development necessary. Asian organisations have always had the best data banks of marketing know-how of Western regions.

To master this development, the participants of a CE have to learn to look beyond the confinements of a restricted area.

The intensive occupation with the culture and civilisation of target markets creates the basis of a deeper understanding.

This is a vital basis for creating bestsellers in other nations and regions.

The absorption of several cultures creates people who think and feel more complex.

This is an important competitive advantage.

The Internet offers daily communication with people of all target areas.

You have to select target groups of particular professional interest.

Step by step the reading of high quality literature will reveal to you the soul of another civilisation.

Educating a population to use the business potential of other nations is a very valuable alternative to emigration with all its frustrations.

The comprehensive use of the business potential of the near and the faraway worlds can reduce the necessity of migration. Migration may often reduce your presence in your home to a short holiday.

14 HIGHER QUALITY OF LIFE BY SELECTION FROM THE MENU OF OTHER CULTURES AND CIVILISATIONS

The integration of cultural achievements, wisdom, meditation and spiritualism of other cultures and civilisations makes life much richer and improves life quality. It is an eternal source of enjoyment which everybody can afford.

The Roman civilisation has absorbed the Greek civilisation. The Greek civilisation has borrowed from the Babylonian culture. The Chinese civilisation has enriched the Japanese culture.

These examples show that it makes great sense to enrich the quality of life by borrowing exciting elements from other cultures.

The booming nations will enjoy many of the pleasures which have been close to our heart.

We have to say good-bye to the more expensive sections of leisure time.

Alternatives have to replace the lost enjoyments. The global cultures offer thousands of very interesting activities. Most of them are inexpensive and can be enjoyed by everybody.

At the same time many new jobs are created by promoting and teaching these activities.

The discovery of many features of foreign civilisations creates above all jobs which are mostly far more pleasant than the previous ones.

By following these steps we create a more sophisticated society.

The relentless drive for more personal money and the unlimited greed for money could be better controlled.

We cannot allow that preditary capitalists turn the world into a desert.

**A CE should promote responsibility
to protect the precious remaining resources of nature.**

15   CONSERVATION OF WORKS OF ART AND MONUMENTS OF CULTURE

Western nations are very rich in culture and civilisations. For future generations and civilisations it is very important to preserve the cultural heritage.

This is a natural field of action for a CE. It can offer preservation at far more competitive prices than the First Economy.

This allows a much larger realm of preservation.

Fine historic buildings could be restored and used as a business platform for companies of the First Economy or the CE.

The Internet-motivated economy allows a greater choice of flexibility for company head offices or branches.

Other buildings could be restored for housing in style. The sense of common property which is privately used for an agreed period of time has to be promoted in a CE.

The rotation system which allows a number of families to live in style for a period of time is preferable.

The systematic promotion of values of civilisation supports tourism.

It has to be considered that mobility will suffer if the evolution from the petrol-driven car to the electric car takes much longer than anticipated.

Marketing of cultural objects and values creates very job intensive activities.

An incredible variety of job activities is possible.

This ranges from the creation of cultural products to the revival of historic music.

**An international marketing knowlege in this field
is certainly essential.**

16   INTERCHANGE BETWEEN RELIGIONS

An intensive interchange of good ideas has enriched religions during many centuries.

These influences have created globally marketable products and concepts.

They have been consolation for souls and minds of the underprivileged slaves and serfs.

On earth they were like cattle to their masters.

They were the basis of the wealth and wellbeing for them.

They could be sold like cattle to provide quick cash for their masters.

Religion promised them rich rewards in the after-life.

In their everyday-life they had only to experience misery.

The development of powerful religious establishments made religions more and more rigid and inbred.

Fine ideas from outside were not used or integrated anymore.

People were to remain embedded in the religion and civilisation of their origin.

Civilisation is as well deeply influenced by religious thoughts.

Fine ideas and philosophies of other religions can enrich life and consciousness of Western people.

Their respect for life and the concept of living in harmony with nature has to be considered as prime condition for a survial strategy.

The broadening of mind to see our actions with the eyes of victims will enduce us to find compromise solutions.

17   LIFE OPPORTUNITIES AND WELFARE FOR OUR FELLOW CREATURES

Our Western political systems have always shown a breathtaking greed by the rich and mighty to destroy the beauties of nature and to turn the flora and fauna of entire countries and continents into money for a chosen few.

The destruction of entire races, the wealth of virgin forests and the destruction of the fauna of the oceans is continuing till today.

Brutality and cruelty still rule the world.

Reckless powerful people are prepared to destroy the climate of this world.

A CE can make a significant contribution to give nature a new chance.

Plants and animals have their own system of intelligence.

It would be an exciting field of activities to discover these secrets.

Doors will be opened to develop many new fields of job creation.

It is certainly an interesting experiment to create communities who live in harmony with nature.

A society which treats the life of animals and plants with the same dignity as some Asian religions do will have their individual interesting developments.

The potential of many thousand plants in the virgin forests have not yet been researched and exploited.

A CE can counteract the destructive activities of the rich and mighty.

They can develop areas where nature receives a new chance.

Living in harmony with nature
can create a new dimension in the lives of many people
and improve their quality of life considerably.

18   LIVING IN HARMONY WITH NATURE OR EXPLOITING AND DESTROYING IT THROUGH PREDATORY CAPITALISM ?

Living in harmony with nature increases life quality. Man has to live in harmony with nature to ensure his long-term survival.

Living in close relationship with nature opens up new dimensions of deep enjoyment.

Some spiritutally-minded people even make considerable progress in communicating with old trees and animals.

Exploring the energy fields of other living beings on planet earth is certainly a worthwhile and highly enjoyable field of meditation.

The vast majority of people is good-natured and will enjoy giving most creatures the right to live.

They will respect the inter-relationship and dependence of all creatures on earth.

There is always a ruthless, cruel minority who is prepared to endless destruction, pilferage and genocides to please their lust and greed for mountains of money.

Today they destroy the green lung of the earth which has often existed for millions of years.

Their predatory mind does not care whether thousands of animals and plants will disappear forever.

They fish the oceans empty with their factory ships. Even the whale with his outstanding intelligence receives no mercy.

They even grind highly intelligent fishes to fish meal for consumption by cattle.

Of course, man has been a cruel cannibal for millions of years. These genes are still dominant in a minority.

This minority has to controlled by the vast majority in the interest of the survival of mankind.

ECONOMIC

ASPECTS

1   GLOBALIZATION OF INDUSTRIAL JOBS

In the past, industrial enterprises had a national identity.

The creation of jobs for their countrymen was an important motivation.

In a globalized world, these honorable traditions are of dwindling consideration.

Today the success with the booming economies of Asia plays a key role.

This happens according to the British proverb:

"If you cannot beat your enemies, join them."

When the Board of Directors changes their objectives, the armies of workers and employees are a disturbing cost factor.

Loyalty and life-long employment belong to another planet.

Traditional values of labour would become irrealistic dreams in a society where you can obtain outstanding results with € 400 monthly.

No resistance is made when 16-hour-shifts are required.

The war economy in peace times of the Chinese is confronted with the comfortable leasure time-oriented life style of Western countries.

It is, of course, totally clear who will be the winner in the end.

Western industrialists often follow the temptation of the Chinese to change sides and join the winners.

**Western workers and employees have to overcome
their present looser concept
and have to organize themselves in a more successful way.**

2   PARTICIPATION IN BOOM MARKETS

The financial currents of our Western world have changed dramatically.Many of yesterday's financial currents bypass the Western countries.

Some very successful hard-working nations have succeeded in transferring millions of jobs and entire industries to their countries.

A CE has to accept these dramatic changes

A substantial part of its income has to derive from the boom economies.

The Internet is an ideal tool to reach these markets in other parts of the world.

Chinese structures already reach every Département in France or any County in the US or the UK.

They can serve as a good example to develop any distant boom market.

The financial resources will be limited at first.

Regions and markets have to be carefully selected. Developing a region in depth will be advantageous.

You have to create a lasting presence in a region.

You will be challenged by Chinese competitors all the time.

This competition has to be beaten by better marketing ideas and concepts.

You have to acquire an excellent marketing knowledge of faraway markets to create bestsellers.

These efforts are difficult but very important since they enable you to grow at the speed of boom markets.

With your marketing you have to observe the trends in boom markets.

They may sometimes have an evolution at amazing speed.

3   MARKETING AND PRODUCTION FOR EXPORT MARKTETS

The changes in other parts of the world are so immense that our world gets turned upside down.

To counteract these changes requires acts of historic proportions.

Most politicians and media managers see the answer to these challenges in the withdrawal to the cosiness of village life or smaller regions.

The life and fate of rabbits and mice who favour similar solutions show that this approach is very risky.

You fall victim to economic predators.

The situation demands for courage to face this challenge.

The Japanese global success was a shining example of excellent marketing work for countries at the other end of the world.

A CE has to establish data banks for the required marketing knowledge.

The quality of the Japanese marketing information has always been better than the information of local institutions.

They always understood tomorrow's customer needs better than the local companies. The distance of 10.000 km was no obstacle to success.

A CE has to make the necessary efforts to reach or to bypass the same quality level.

There is no easy way to master this challenge.

This is an employment base for thousands of people
with a creative mind.

Information is an essential basis for success.

The challenge is to turn defeat into success step by step.

The quality of information is a key tool
to turn the tide.

4 USE OF INTERNET AND MODERN COMMUNICATION

Internet Marketing is a very important tool which enables a CE to develop global opportunities.

The Western world has its roots in the colonial and European dominance of the world.

This is now fading away, and the financial currents are turning to the up and coming markets.

The participants of a CE have to follow the new directions of the financial currents. They cannot stick to the old ways.

We have to accept the Chinese global marketing system as a shining example and develop an alternative system.

A CE is not burdened with the illusion of Western superiority.

They accept the fact that the Chinese and other economies have bypassed us.

The time has come for us to benefit from many fine ideas of the financially very successful players in the global economy.

Global Internet Marketing requires the study of foreign languages and cultures and their business customs.

It offers job opportunities for thousands who are prepared to accept the challenges of a new world.

Repetitive jobs are for machines. The majority has to accept jobs where mental and intellectual capacities play an important role.

Chinese institutions make great efforts to learn the new developments in other industrial countries and to benefit from the intellectual work of all nations.

**A CE has to learn from them and
to benefit from all new Chinese developments.**

5   FINANCING PRODUCT DEVELOPMENTS

Happiness, success and full employment for all members are the most important objectives of a CE.

Capital will be of short supply for a long period of time.

All Asian economical systems were faced with the same challenges.

A CE has to apply the Asian strategies to reduce costs and to reach its objectives.

By integrating the successes of Chinese product developments, years of R&D work can be spared.

A Chinese-style growth can be envisaged and achieved.

Western rules can be suicidal when faced with an opponent of this power and ambition.

It is important that the Chinese competitor feels the breath of the CE down its neck.

This improves the consciousness to be a worthy opponent.

It opens the opportunity to achieve Chinese speed of progress.

The CE receives an improved opportunity to close the increasing gap between Chinese and Western economical growth.

We have to integrate Asian-motivated working methods to heal the wounds which the dieing process of many Western industries have opened.

6   PROFIT OPTIMIZATION - MEGA PROFITS

The Western world is fading away quicker than anticipated.

Slavery, enforced drug consumption, the pilferage of the prosperity of subdued nations have created millions of victims and immense prosperity.

This enabled a rich minority to enforce their system upon the rest of the world.

Gold-based currencies may be fine for a chosen few with often inhuman and reckless business methods.

The decendants of good honest people must get a chance as well. They deserve it probably more than the occupants of castles and manor houses.

They had no opportunity to pilfer the wealth of nations with inferior military equipment.

The value and dignity of human labour has to be revived.

A growth economy has to emerge to convert the will, need and capacity to earn a living into the realization of private and public works as well as the creation of thousands of products and services.

The development of the past few years has shown that Western industrialists have very little or no loyalty to their staff who have created their prosperity.

Profit optimization induces them to get rid of their loyal labour force just like discarding useless junk.

Life gets much easier if you operate with low-cost labour.

The sacrificed labour forces have to create their own solutions to regain human dignity.

The First Economy should support their effort.

7   FINANCIAL COMPETITIVNESS

Chinese structures have been operating with political prices for many years.

Important cost factors like e. g. Pension costs could be transferred to other production places which were not involved in global competition.

The Western system of plant-linked costing often proved to be suicidal.

The situation requires that these competitors have to be beaten with their own strategies.

A CE allows a greater flexibility than the First Economy to meet such challenges.

Social costs have to be carried by productions specializing in local products.

Products for global markets should be exempt from social costs or reduced to an absolute minimum. This should be considered in the social cost share.

The challenge of the CE is to create a great number of jobs for the unfortunate who have been rationalized away by the First Economy.

In many cases, they will suffer the fate of eternal unemployment.

With a shrinking employment basis, this will be a great burden for the tax payer.

This will get more and more unbearable, or entire industries are transferred to the cheap labour economies.

China has always refused any step to give the Yuan an exchange value which is related to its purchasing power.

Undervaluing the Yuan has always been an essential part of their global success strategy.

The CE has to learn from this essential part of the very impressive Chinese economical expansion.

A currency solution has to be found to make your products globally very competitive.

Chinese Authorities have been defending the Yuan exchange rates with great passion. The Yuan exchange rate was a pillar of their never-ending success story.

Maybe permission is given to establish a local currency. Alternatively staff has to work with project-linked wage reductions.

The staff has to make a major success possible.

**This will create the ideal success and
survival base for global operations.**

8   USING THE SUCCESS FORMULAE OF THE OPPONENT

Asian structures have developed strategies which often proved to be lethal for their competitors.

Many structures are based on the tight co-operation structures on a national scale.

A CE is a much smaller player.

It has to modify Asian success strategies to its dimensions.

The Chinese Internet Marketing activity reaches every region in every target market.

Their regional activities are often better organized than those of local suppliers.

A thorough Internet Marketing activity can start in selected regions.

It will take some time to achieve a global activity such as Chinese structures have organized.

Such a structure could be offered to all CE's.

A first-class service for the global community will create a large number of highly qualified jobs and is an intellectual challenge.

A CE will have a shortage of capital for a long while.

The Managers of a CE have to benefit from the superior wealth of the opponents.

Absorbing Chinese developments and improving them will have to be the business basis for a long time.

This is an important advantage to save time and money.

You can go into production and marketing very quickly.

It is always important to learn from the opponents and to apply their success strategies.

Concentrating the activities of one industry or craft in one region or town will speed up progress.

The distribution over an entire country or continent will not allow the results to assure survival.

SOCIAL

ASPECTS

1 THE ROOTS OF WEALTH

Russian and Western European aristocrats have measured their wealth in the number of slaves and unpaid serfs who were entrusted to them.

Their amazing wealth and the splendor of their castles had the unpaid labour of serfs as a basis.

When serfs became workers and employees the splendor faded away as it was then no longer possible to maintain a 128-bedroom castle.

Industrialists followed in the footsteps of aristocrats.

The average millionaire has the ambition to become a multi-millionaire. The systematic reduction of labour costs is an essential part on the road to a multi-millionaire status.

The fate of slaves and serfs was never a concern of their masters. The wellbeing of their workers and employees would not cause a sleepless night to the heirs of industrial enterprises.

The pressure of Asian competition forces them either to benefit from Asian wages or to use every possibility and every way to reduce the income of their straff.

The Asian challenge is primarily a technological one. If we do not make extreme efforts they will be a generation ahead of us.

In practical terms, this means that Western wages have to become lower than Asian wages.

Labour unions have to fight to get prices down to Asian level.

Wage increase is not in line with today's and tomorrow's world.

China has the medium-term objective to take today's position of the West.

They endeavour to become the sun around which our planet revolves.

If we are honest: This is the natural role of an industrialized China.

The factory of the world claims the role to be our economical sun.

2   DEMOGRAPHIC DEVELOPMENT

The demographic development has a close relationship to the economic success and the availability of jobs.

The availability of jobs and the opportunity to earn good money releases the imagination of hundreds of thousands, millions and even hundreds of millions.

If the CE is trying harder than the management of the old traditional industries and succeeds in creating many jobs, people will come in any quantity in search of work.

All you have to do is to select those families who have many children and create a climate to take the responsibility for larger families. and the problem is on the way of being solved.

We have to accept that our past values will be fading away.

Our successful industries of the past will become too slow for today's world.

Even smaller and medium-sized companies will not find enough business in the vicinity.

The systematic creative business development in well-selected regions of the global village becomes vital for economic survival.

A CE has to accept the responsibility of becoming a job creation machine.

The values of the rich and ruthless have to be replaced by the values of a more human economic society .

The reality of trying harder becomes, however, essential for survival and success.

The creation of a CE opens the unique chance for the revival of an economic Renaissance.

We all will have to accept that the comparatively easy times will probably never come back.

We have to find a new place in the concert of hard-working people.

3   RELENTLESS EFFORT FOR MARKET EXPANSION

A relentless marketing effort is the most important pre-condition for long-term success.

A longer period of rest works out as the start of an economic decline.

The speed of progress in China and other Asian countries forces even a CE to a higher speed in market development.

It is very important that the cosy Western way of life is buried and forgotten.

Chinese industries have saved decades of product development and thousands of millions US-$ in investment by copying Western technology.

The CE's are well advised to follow their example. It is the only way to get some of the jobs back which got lost to the Chinese copying efforts.

It is important to analyse the Chinese marketing, product development and production efforts and to absorb the useful elements.

A CE has no great prestige to defend. It can tune itself to the same speed of progress. This may not provide the optimisation of comfort.

The wisdom of Darwin about the survival of the fittest is of key importance.

In the long run the CE has to fill the gaps which have opened due to the fact that many industrialists changed sides.

In past decades it was sufficient to appoint one distributor per country. This was, of course, the lazy man's way to riches.

In today's world you have to reach each potential major customer to progress at the same speed as your main challengers.

This means in real terms that you have to use the Internet to contact 300 or 400 companies instead of one.

**A greater success will be the reward
for your efforts.**

4   RELENTLESS CREATION OF NEW JOB OPPORTUNITIES

China is succeeding in its ambition to be the R&D section and the factory of the world.

An industrialized China of 1,4 million people will fix the price level and the R&D standard for the rest of the world.

The gradual decline of the purchasing power for the vast majority of the population in Western countries forces them to adapt the Chinese price and wage level.

The rest of the economic factors have to follow.

To achieve this flexibility is easier for a CE than for the First Economy.

The CE has to take the level of the Chinese global market penetration as a standard.

You have to start with selected regions and perform a thorough market development.

The market position has to be improved all the time.

The position of a CE is not a position of comfort but an attitude of greater intensity to ensure long-term success and survival.

Inspiration and new ideas to create new jobs and to recognize new job trends can be learned from the professional magazines of the global community.

The achievements of the booming nations are of particular interest.

It is very useful to learn from the few who have been most successful in the global community.

The constant observation of global opportunities and ideas creates the working base for selecting activities which are suitable for the CE.

The search for new opportunities has to be in line with the number of jobs required to achieve full employment.

Full employment is the main objective,
not ultimate profits for a chosen few.

5   JOB SECURITY AND
RELIABLE SOURCES OF INCOME

Job security and reliable sources of income during a lifespan are of utmost importance.

Our present economical system is dominated by the greed of a rich minority.

Many of them have acquired their wealth by ruthlessly destroying the virgin forests of this world, by exterminating native people and robbing their land, by enslaving decent people, by converting decent honest people into serfs.

This way a wage-free society emerged making the owners of serfs and slaves immensely rich.

Even today unemployment is the most frequent source of death. Thousands commit suicide in traffic or on the rails of a subway or railway line when they have lost their job and identity because Chinese workers are much cheaper. Millions die primaturely of grief.

The culprits of this development enjoy their lives on their yachts. The victims are just collaterial damage on their drive to even more money.

In a CE job security must have priority to the accumulation of wealth in a few hands.

In China I have seen 70 and 80 year old craftsmen producing large vases of an incredible grace and beauty.

It would have been a sin to waste their talents.

We have to create activities where our senior people can develop their talents.

In many sections of the economy experience is of greater significance than physical strength.

Sections of the economy have to be reserved for senior people.

Other sections of the economy have to tolerante that senior colleagues achieve 70 or 80 % of the performance of younger specialists.

An intelligent job rotation of senior staff will keep their minds fit and creative.

The learning process should never end.

**The employment of senior people
is one of the great advantages of a CE.**

6 ADMINISTRATION OF NEED

China's industry has integrated 400 million workers. Another thousand are watching the progress with envy.

They see their lucky neighbours enjoying new houses and fine Chinese food. They are becoming more and more impatent to enjoy the same quality of life.

In some places this impatience has already led to social unrest and burning of shops and offices.

The Chinese Authorities are under great pressure to bring the entire population to the new Chinese quality of life-level.

The required speed of progress can only be achieved by transferring Western industries to China.

By the strategy of absorbing Western know-how they arrive at their level without investment of time and money.

With the economized resources they can drive further product development ahead and arrive at a level which is beyond the reach of Western initiators.

It often happens that Chinese patents prevent Western companies from manufacturing their own developments.

They aim at a technological level where the Western countries have to abandon their once flourishing industry.

Another source of Western prosperity has disappeared.

Step by step China enjoys our quality of life.

Our section of the population that makes a living by earning salaries and wages will experience the poverty which the Chinese population once experienced.

The Western decline will take place over a longer period of time.

Charity organisations are making extreme efforts to prevent hunger for growing sections of the community.

Charity will have its limitations.

**We have to act now to create the conditions
and the economic basis
to keep starvation from our doorstep.**

7   LIVELIHOOD FOR PEOPLE IN NEED

Our way of life is most likely to be challenged and destroyed by developments and evolutions which take place at other ends of the world.

They are becoming faster and faster in their product developments.

They have the right products for new market trends when Western industialists still work at their profit optimizsation by repeating mass production of outdated products.

The financial basis by which Western politicians finance their social system is most likely going to erode.

This erosion process has already started.

A certain percentage of citizens will not be able to contribute to the society at old age with their work.

This community has to be kept as small as possible.

The deterioration of mind and body is often a sign of lack of self discipline.

Unhealthy food is often the cause of a premature deterioration of human faculties.

It is certainly justified to place a significant tax on unhealthy products to bring them out of the reach for mass consumption.

The results of wrong nutrition are just as destructive to the ability to earn a living in old age as smoking.

The participants of a CE have to be informed that wrong nutrition can be suicide in instalments.

Some people who are too conservative have to be shocked by negative examples of devastating developments.

It is essential that reason prevails and that they change their course.

The income of the taxes of unhealthy food could be used to maintain that part of the population which has sinned against their health and life expectancy.

The tax should be sufficient to finance the very considerable health and hospital expenses.

EPILOGUE

1   OUTLAWING PREDATORY CAPITALISM

Predatory capitalism has been the course of death for centuries. It still is.

The cruel transfer of industries to cheap labour countries still causes desperation for millions of people.

Salaries and wages are still the source of income for the majority of people.

The transfer of their livelihood to far-away countries destroys families and causes the suicide of thousands.

Transferring thousands of jobs away from the Chinese population is regarded as treason in China. It leads to a penalty from between three years of imprisonment to public execution.

The roots of many older legal systems go back to the time of serfdom and near-slavery. At this time, a rich man could crush the existence of any dependant.

In today's evolution stage the fate and happiness of the working people has to be in the center of all decisions.

Predatory capitalism has to be tamed.

The West cannot afford the luxury of destroying the livelihood of millions to please some predatory capitalists.

Of course, the predatory capitalist will bribe his way.

Moneys earned this way could be confiscated by the community and given to people in need.

A CE can start to make life uncomfortable to predatory capitalists.

2 THE DIRECT ROAD TO HAPPINESS

The principal objective of the First Economy is to provide the means which enable people to purchase their piece of happiness and satisfaction.

This is obviously a detour on the road to win a small section of happiness.

This happiness often lasts as long as a warm stream of cash is coming your way.

If a modification in the fast changing global economy will end the stream of money, your happiness will turn into frustration.

A CE offers the opportunity to embark directly on the way to happiness.

The detour to earn first the means to buy a piece of happiness can be avoided.

The people of giant nations like China and India are on the move to claim their piece of prosperity.

Their labour force is often better educated and is more motivated than the employees and workers in most Western countries.

This will force the population of the West to a new way of life.

They cannot return to the simple and very modest way of life of their fathers.

Circumstances will force them to chose the direct road to happiness.

Happiness has, however, to be less material.

The mental and spiritual aspect of happiness has to be more promoted and developed.

The future has to be conceived and shaped in many creative ways.

ABOUT THE AUTHOR …

Norbert Braun - Certified Industrial Interpreter for English and French, Certified Accountant for Industrial Production, Sales Trainer and Sales Promoter - has been entrusted with very difficult sales missions in many countries around the globe. His outstanding achievements made him "Mr. Mission Impossible" on the sales sector.

In his first book **Die Kompostierung der "Grufties" und "Scheintoten" (Composting the "Buried" and "Nearly Dead")** he describes a Japanese working initiative in which he participated and whose objective it was to create working places for senior people.

Furthermore, he was entrusted with the task of selling Computer-based Learning Software (CBL-SW) to the HQs of Labour Exchanges, Ministries of Labour, Ministries of Science, Regional Administrations and Educational Institutions.

This happened at the time of the re-union of the two Germanies, when many people had to be re-trained to the working methods of the West.

After that a follow-up business was arranged, preferrably in countries with great employment problems, such as China, Russia, Australia, Canada, Northern Spain, France, Great Britain and Ireland.

In his first book, the Author places his know-how and rich experience at the disposal of the inhabitants of dieing economic regions as well as employees and workers of migrating industries in order to enable them to re-conquer a part of their lost standard of living.

In his present work, the Authors offers a way how to achieve a higher quality of life by changing established values.

FURTHER WORKS OF THE AUTHOR

1 Die Kompostierung der "Grufties" und "Scheintoten"

**Ein visionärer Versuch,
wertvolles Humankapital
zum Leben zu erwecken**

**(A visionary attempt
to restore precious human capital)**

2 Bruttosozialglück statt Raubtierkapitalismus

**Ein Versuch,
der wirtschaftlichen Götterdämmerung
des Westens entgegenzuwirken**

**(Original Version of:
Gross National Happiness versus
Predatory Capitalism)**